P9-CAZ-039

Living and Learning

Program Authors

Connie Juel, Ph.D.

Jeanne R. Paratore, Ed.D.

Deborah Simmons, Ph.D.

Sharon Vaughn, Ph.D.

Glenview, Illinois
Boston, Massachusetts
Chandler, Arizona
Hoboken, New Jersey

ISBN-13: 978-0-328-45280-4
ISBN-10: 0-328-45280-7

10 11 12 13 14 V011 18 17 16 15 14
CC1

Living and Learning

Trying New Things

What can we learn by trying new things?

Let's Make a Trade

How can we get what we need without money?

Smart Saving 57

How can we achieve goals?

Wants and Needs 83

How do we get what we want and need?

KID Business 109

How can kids earn money?

Trying New Things

Trying New Things

Let's Explore

Words 2 the Wise

The world is full of fun things to see and do. As you read, think about what you can learn by **trying new things.**

Let's Explore

TRYING NEW THINGS

Pam is learning to go up this rock. Pam puts one hand in a space and pulls up. Then Pam puts her other hand in a space and pulls up. Step by step Pam gets up the rock. Pam steps up, up, up. When will Pam get to the top?

Can you build a ship? Bill builds lots of them. He puts much effort into his ships so that they will not sink. Bill makes his ships out of this and that. Then Bill fills a tub and tests them. Which ship will be the best?

Tap, tap, TAP! Tap, tap, TAP! Lin is learning to drum. She listens to her friend drum. Then Lin drums. When Lin gets good, she will drum with other children in a band. It will be fun!

Ken attends a class about space at the community center. Ken learns when the moon changes and what makes Earth spin. He learns that the sun is hot, hot, hot. When class ends, Ken looks up and asks, "Which star is that, and that, and that?"

AT THE COMMUNITY CENTER

by Rebecca Ramirez
illustrated by Margeaux Lucas

What is a community center? Who can use it?
And what can you learn there?

A community center is a spot where kids, moms, and dads can get together. Lots of people can use the center. They can attend classes and learn new things. They can get fit. Kids can go to camp and be in clubs.

Which class will we take?

People can pick from long lists of classes at the community center. What do moms want to learn? What do dads like? Kids can take classes too. Which class would you pick? You can think it over.

Ben and his mom and dad have fun in classes. His mom picked a singing class. His dad picked a computer class. Ben is learning to act and help put on plays. Ben will even bring his dog Mugs to dog class. Mugs will learn to walk well with Ben and to sit.

Let's get fit!

How can kids get fit? Ben can get fit at his community center. He can jump and run and kick.

Moms and dads can get fit as well. Mom runs on a track. Dad swims laps. It takes effort to get fit, but it is fun!

Some community centers run camps when school is out and Mom and Dad work. Camps can help kids get fit. Ben and his pals swam and fished at camp.

How about a club?

Some centers have clubs for kids. Ben is in a club that learns about bugs. His pal is in a club that learns how to build things. One day Ben will get in the chess club.

Which club would you pick?

Get the facts!

Has this list of classes, camps, and clubs got you thinking? Get on the Web and get facts from your community center. Then get in and have fun!

What Do You Think?

What can kids and moms and dads do at a community center?

BUILDING A BAT HOUSE

by Candyce Norvell

illustrated by Maurie Manning

"This is it, Dad," Jem said. "This is the class we picked. The clock says 6:45. Can we go in?"

Dad checked his watch. Then Jem and Dad went in.

Dad and Jem attend classes at the community center. They take classes and learn new things. In this class, Dad and Jem will learn about bats. Then they will build a bat house.

Dad and Jem looked around. "How will we build a bat house?" asked Jem. "Will it be big? Will bats like it?"

Dad said, "That man will tell us about bats. Then we can build a house that fits a bat."

At the class, Jem and Dad learned much about bats. Bats have wings but are not birds. Bats eat lots of bugs. Bats come out at dusk to hunt for bugs. And bats like a snug little house in the day.

Jem and Dad learned about building too. Jem handed Dad parts and Dad cut them. Jem held the parts and Dad put them together. Then Jem held the brush as Dad held the can. It took much effort to build a bat house.

When the bat house was done, Dad looked at Jem. "I think bats will like this bat house," he said. "Once it is set up, bats can go in and out as they hunt for bugs at dusk."

Jem shut her eyes. "Yes, I can picture that, Dad."

The next day, Dad set up the bat house. "This bat house
must get lots of sun," he said. "Bats like it hot."

Just then, a red bird went up and sat on the house. "This
house is not for a bird," said Jem with a grin. "It is just
for bats."

At dusk, Jem and Dad went out. "Look up, Jem. A bat is at the new house."

Jem looked up. "We did it! We made a house for bats! What can we build next?"

Dad did not have to think. "Let us go back to the community center and find out!"

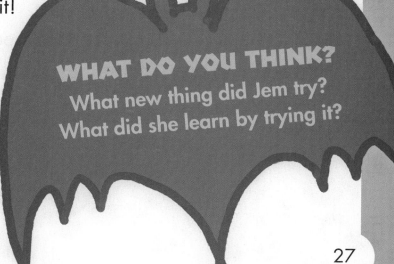

WHAT DO YOU THINK?
What new thing did Jem try? What did she learn by trying it?

Lewis Has a Trumpet

by Karla Kuskin

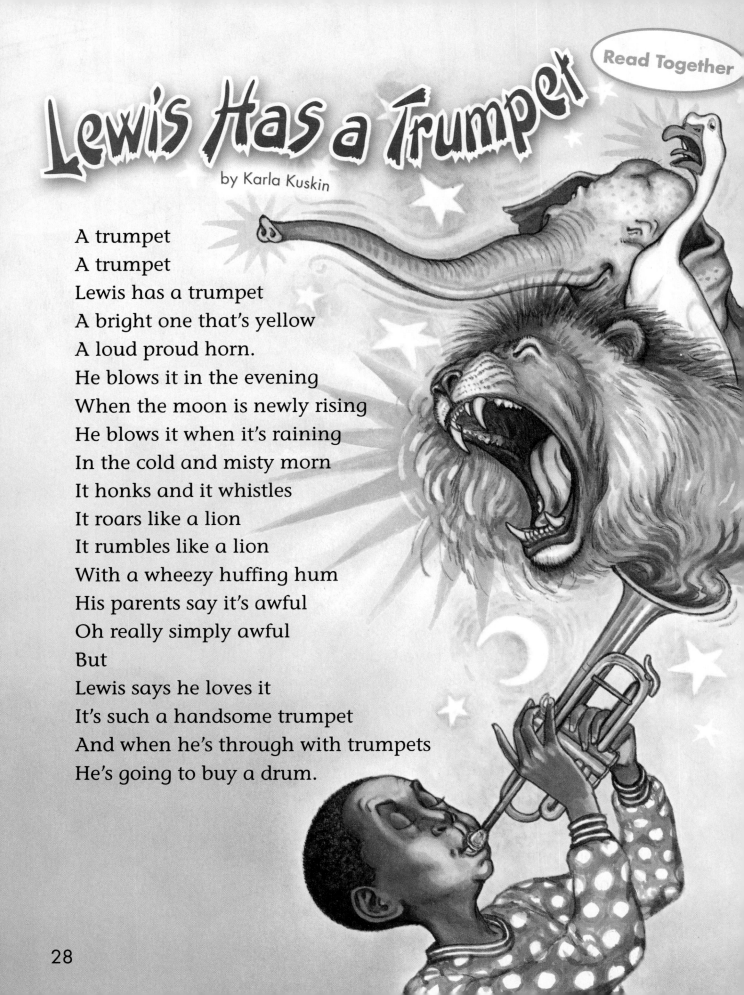

A trumpet
A trumpet
Lewis has a trumpet
A bright one that's yellow
A loud proud horn.
He blows it in the evening
When the moon is newly rising
He blows it when it's raining
In the cold and misty morn
It honks and it whistles
It roars like a lion
It rumbles like a lion
With a wheezy huffing hum
His parents say it's awful
Oh really simply awful
But
Lewis says he loves it
It's such a handsome trumpet
And when he's through with trumpets
He's going to buy a drum.

Crazy Boys

by Beverly McLoughland

Watching buzzards,
Flying kites,
Lazy, crazy boys
The Wrights. They

Tried to fly
Just like a bird
Foolish dreamers
Strange. Absurd. We

Scoffed and scorned
Their dreams of flight
But we were wrong
And they were Wright.

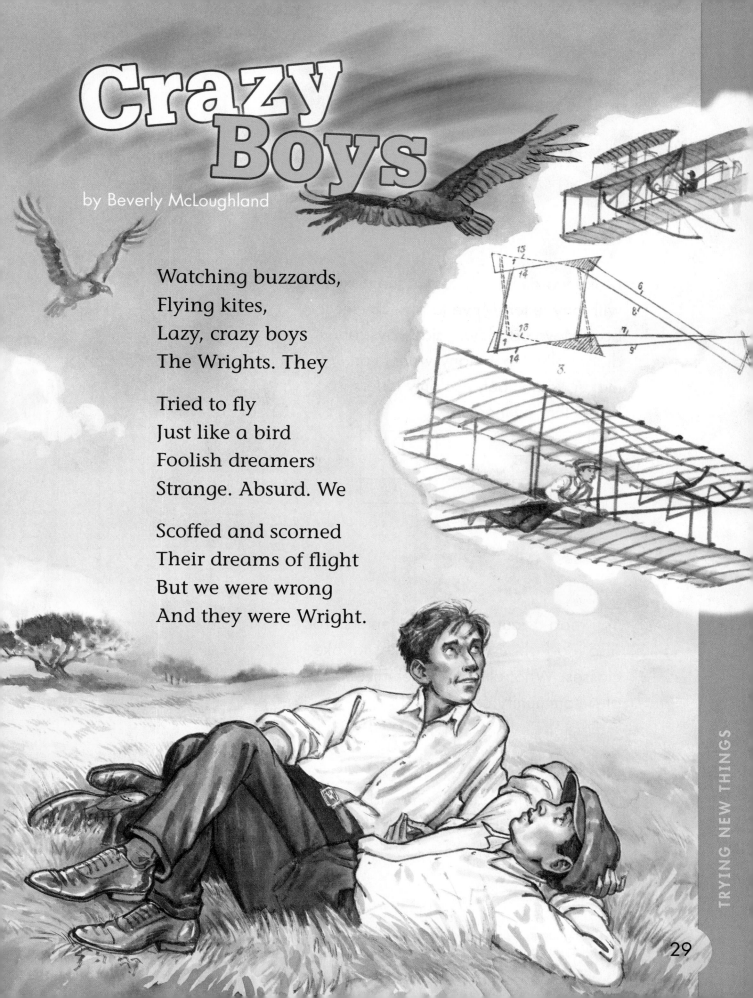

4 You 2 Do

Word Play

Make words from letters in the boxes. Start with any letter. Move to any connecting box. Move up, down, sideways, or diagonally. How many words can you make? Remember, use only letters in boxes that connect.

B	E	D
U	A	N
T	I	P

Making Connections

You read about community centers. You also read about Jem, who likes to take classes. What else might Jem like to do at a community center?

On Paper

Which new thing that you read about would you most like to try? Write about why you would like to try it.

Possible answers for Word Play: bed, but, tub, bad, dab, tip, pit, pin, pan, pad, den, end, and, pain, pane, bead, bean, bat, bait, neat

Let's Make a Trade

Contents

Let's Make a Trade

32

Words 2 the Wise

Someone gives and someone takes. That's what **trading** is all about. As you read, think about the trades people make.

GIVE

Lots of people like to trade. People can trade old things for new things. They do not have to use money. Did you ever trade with a pal? What did you trade? What did you give? What did you get?

34

AND TAKE

Jane and Steve have jobs at home. Jane takes out the trash. Steve makes the beds. Jane and Steve trade jobs. Now Jane will make beds. Steve will take out trash.

35

Kids trade for things they do not have. Dave has two packs of grape gum. Mike has a white kite. Is one kite worth two packs of gum? They trade. Would you want gum or a kite?

Lots of people like to trade. Moms trade. Dads trade. Kids trade with pals. It is fun for them to give and to take.

TRIBES AND TRADES

by Jerrill Parham • illustrated by Albert Lorenz

Long ago, these people were part of a tribe. They fished in a huge lake. They picked up shells in the sand. They hunted and set traps. They made crafts. They had shells and bones to use in these crafts.

This community had lots of things. But they did not have money. They did not use money to get things they lacked.* What did this tribe do? They had to trade. What could they trade?

* **lacked** did not have

This tribe had lots of fish. They had animal skins as well. These fish and skins were their goods. These were the goods they could trade. They could trade them for rice. Rice was a thing they lacked.

They had to go a long way to get rice. So they packed their goods to bring with them. First they packed skins and fish. Then they chose shells to bring as gifts. At last they set out on their trip.

They went down a path that animals had made. It went past pine trees and white rocks. It went up hills and across flat land. At times they met other tribes. These tribes had goods to trade as well.

At last they got to the place to trade
for rice. They met the tribe that had rice.
"Tum, bong, tum!" A boy hit a red drum.
It was time to trade!

The tribe with skins chose five bags of rice. The tribe with rice chose one big skin. One big skin was worth five bags of rice. The tribes made the swap. "Tum, bong, tum!" Both tribes felt glad. Both tribes had goods they could use.

Then the tribes sat around a fire. They made up tales to share. Then they made one last trade. The tribe with skins gave their gift of shells. The tribe with rice made a gift of the red drum. "Tum, bong, tum!"

What Do You Think?

What did the tribe with skins do to get rice?
List the steps they took.

A Trade Is a

by Ashe North

illustrated by Lindy Burnett

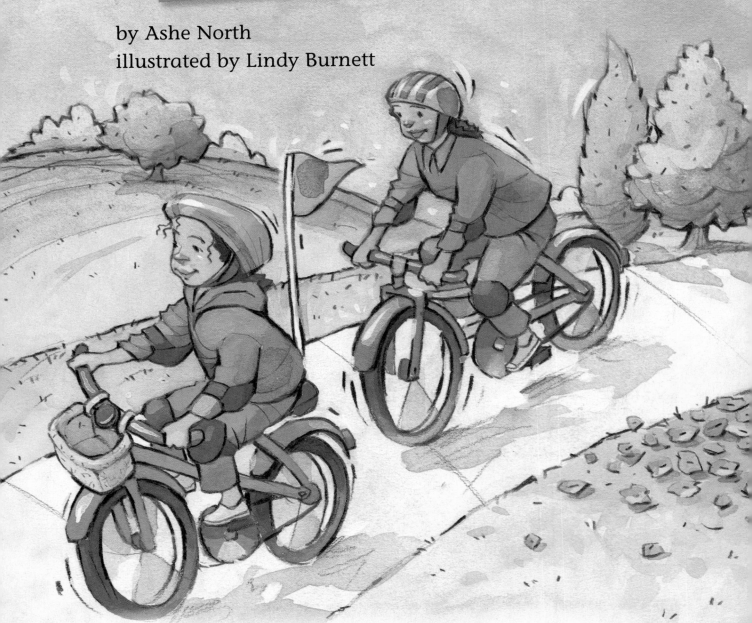

Gen likes to ride her bike. As she rides, her bike flag flaps in the wind. It goes swish, flap, swish.

One day, Gen went on a bike ride with her mom. They rode past Dane and his pal. Dane had a nice kite.

Trade

"That is a nice red kite, Dane," said Gen. "It goes up a long way!"

"I like that flag," said Dane. "It waves in the wind!"

Gen had a big smile. "Do you think that kite is worth the same as this flag? We can trade!"

The next day, Gen and Dad went on a bike ride.
Gen said, "I wish I had my flag."

Dad looked at Gen. "A trade is a trade, Gen." Gen
felt bad for a while. Then she saw June on the steps.

"Those pens are nice, June," said Gen.
June said, "I like these pens, but I wish I had that kite!"
Gen had a big smile. "Do you think that those pens are worth as much as this kite? We can swap!"

Before lunch Gen and Kate had to shop for milk. Gen said, "It was fun to trade twice. But I still miss my flag a little bit. I like how it went swish, flap, swish."

"Sis, a trade is a trade," Kate said.

Then Gen met Grace. Grace had some very cute mice to use on a stage!

"Those are cute mice, Grace. I like that one with its big, pink nose!" said Gen.

Grace said, "I like those pens, Gen. Do you think that five mice are worth ten pens? We can swap!"

Gen rode away with the mice. "The pens were nice, but these mice are so cute! I am glad that I did not have to spend money to get them."

Then Gen saw Dane. A huge truck sat in front of his home. Dane was packing.

"That big flag will not fit in that box, Dane. But these mice will fit. Will you trade?" asked Gen.

Now Gen was glad that a trade is a trade. The flag made her bike look just like it looked before. It went swish, flap, swish!

What Do You Think?

Name the trades that Gen made from first to last. Which swap did she like best?

TRADING ON THE SILK ROAD

Long ago, people traveled on the Silk Road to trade. Play this Silk Road game with a partner. Use a button for each player and a number cube. Roll the cube and move that number of spaces. If you land on a space with a number, follow the instructions. If you get to Constantinople first, you win!

1 Your camels are loaded with silks. Roll again.

2 The desert is hot and dry. Get out fast! Move ahead two.

3 Stop to trade for food and water. Miss a turn.

4 You are stuck in the mountains. Miss a turn.

5 Bandits rob you. Go back two.

6 Trade for carpets and spices. Miss a turn.

7 You reached Constantinople. You win!

4 YOU 2 DO

Word Play

These kids trade for things that rhyme.
Tell what they can get.

Mike has a **dime.** He trades it for a ___.
Hint: It's green.

Gene has a **rose.** He trades it for a ___.
Hint: It sprays water.

Kate has a **snake.** She trades it for a ___.
Hint: It tastes sweet.

Luke has a **cane.** He trades it for a ___.
Hint: It can fly.

Making Connections

Work with a partner to make two lists.
On one, list how Gen's trades were like
the tribes' trades. On the other, list how
they were different.

On Paper

Write about a trade you would like to
make. What would you trade? What
might you get?

Answers for Word Play: dime—lime; rose—hose;
snake—cake; cane—plane or crane

Smart Saving

Contents

Smart Saving

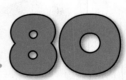

Words 2 the Wise

What do people do when they want something but don't have enough money to buy it? They save! Think about how **smart saving** helps people reach their goals.

Let's Explore

Saving and Spending

Ben is like lots of kids. He gets cash from gifts, jobs, and an allowance. He saves his money, spends it, and gives some to help others.

Ben shakes his bank. "This bank is heavy. I have lots of cash!"

Ben shakes his bank again. His money spills on his bed. Ben makes piles. He adds them up. Ben lists the amount in his book. Then he takes the cash to a bank. Ben hands his money to a man at the bank. The cash is a deposit. It is added to his savings.

At times, Ben wishes for expensive things such as a bike and games. Ben has to save up for a long time to get things like those.

Ben will do nice things with his money too. He will give some of his savings to help people.

Tim helps.

Matt helps.

Jen helps.

Kids like Ben have savings plans. They save for things. They use savings to help people too.

Tim sends cash to help build homes for kids. Matt uses his to help schools plant trees. Jen helps pets get homes.

Do you have a savings plan? What would you save for?

SMART SAVING

Put It in the BANK

by Annie Bird
illustrated by Ronnie Rooney

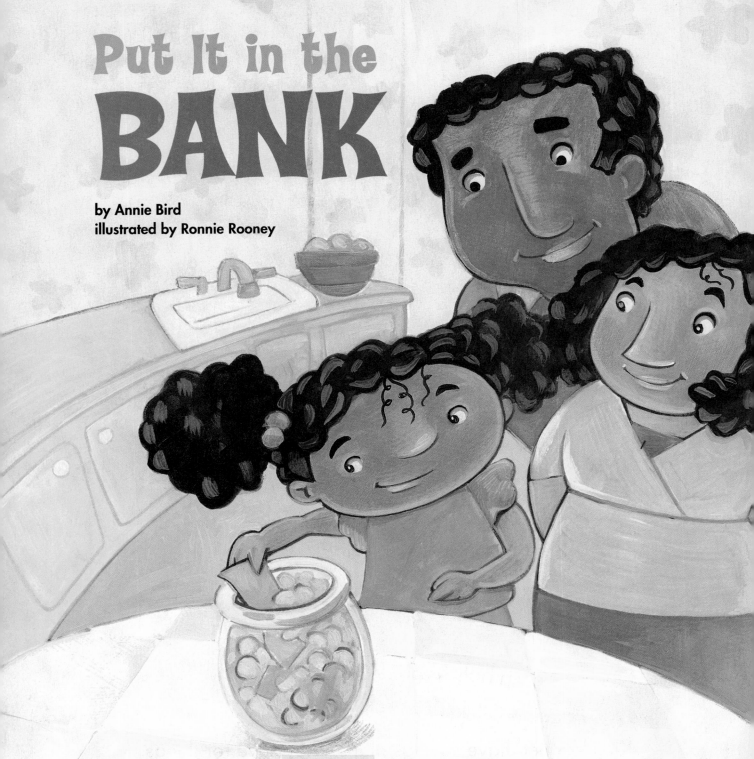

Some kids save allowance. Some kids spend it. Beth is one of those kids who wanted to save it. She had some wishes. Beth wished to get some expensive things.

"If you wish to get those things," Mom and Dad told Beth, "just save, save, save!"

When Mom and Dad gave Beth an allowance, guess what she did with it? Beth stuck that money in her big, glass bank. And now that big, glass bank was filled to the brim with lots of cash. Bills spilled over the top.

"Mom and Dad," yelled Beth. "I can not fit another cent in this old bank of mine. What can I do? What fixes can I make?"

"It is time for a new bank," said Dad. "Pack that cash in some boxes."

Mom, Dad, and Beth went to a big bank next to the community center.

"Can I help you?" Miss Ashes asked them.

"This is Beth," said Mom.

"Beth wishes to put her savings here," said Dad.

67

Beth handed Miss Ashes her boxes of cash. "I have lots of dimes and bunches of bills in these boxes."

"I will add this up and make a deposit for you," said Miss Ashes. "You can make deposits and add to your savings any time. You can take cash out of your savings too."

"How will I know how much cash I have?" Beth asked. Miss Ashes spoke. "I am glad Beth is asking that. Banks can track how much money you have. When you want to know the amount, I can print it out. I will print it now and Beth can take it."

Beth had a huge smile on her face. "Thanks for helping me, Miss Ashes. I will save lots in this bank. I can deposit my allowance. I can save for expensive things. And I will know how much cash I have because the bank will track the amount in my savings."

Then Beth gave Mom and Dad big hugs. "This is a fine savings plan," Beth said. "Now I know what I will do with my money. I will put it in the bank."

What Do You Think?

What was Beth's savings plan?

BANK ON IT!

by Seth Hawks • illustrated by Melanie Seigel

Mike and Rob are best pals who work together. Today they helped Miss Getz plant roses.

Miss Getz handed money to Mike and Rob. "You boys worked well," she said. "You did a fine job planting and watering."

"Thanks," they said.

On the way home, the boys passed a shop.
"Check out that skate deck!* I could do kick flips on that!" said Rob.

Mike saw the price tag. "That skate deck is way too expensive!"

*skate deck the flat part of a skateboard

"That skate deck is expensive," said Rob. "But wishes will not help me get it. From now on, I am going to save my cash. I will deposit it in a safe place."

Rob got boxes, news print, and tape. He made a bank to save his money.

Rob slid two dimes in the bank. The bank blinked. Then it came to life! It was jumping and twisting!

"Huh?" said Rob.

The bank sang, "Clink, clank, clink, clank! Put your savings in this bank!" Then it was still* once again.

***still** quiet

75

The next day, Mike and Rob helped Doctor Lim. They took five huge boxes to the trash. She gave them ten dimes.

"I will get a big drink," said Mike.

"Not me," said Rob. "I am holding on to this money. I plan to save the whole amount for that skate deck."

Rob put his dimes in the thin slot on his bank. The bank jumped up and spun around. It sang the same song. Rob held up his hand. "Shush!" he said.

Mike and Rob had many jobs for many bosses. Mike did not save. Mike spent. Rob would deposit his cash in his bank. He wanted that skate deck!

At last, Rob took his savings out of his bank. He had a huge amount of cash. Did he save enough?

Rob went to the shop. He checked the price tag on the skate deck. Rob added up his savings. He had enough! Rob gave his cash to the man in the shop. The bank winked at Rob. Rob winked back.

WHAT DO YOU THINK?

What steps did Rob take to get enough money for the skate deck?

PENNY POWER!

Would you rather have a penny doubled every day for a month or one million dollars?

A penny a day is only seven cents a week! But doubling the pennies each day gives you much, much more. This is how it works.

Week 1

	Start With	Double It	Now You Have
Sunday	$.01	1+1	$ .02
Monday	$.02	2+2	$ .04
Tuesday	$.04	4+4	$ .08
Wednesday	$.08	8+8	$ .16
Thursday	$.16	16+16	$ .32
Friday	$.32	32+32	$ .64
Saturday	$.64	64+64	$1.28

After one week you'll have $1.28. That's not a lot of money. But remember, you should double your pennies each day for a month. Look at the calendar to see what happens.

Sunday	Monday	Tuesday	Wednesday	Thursday	Friday	Saturday
1 $.02	**2** $.04	**3** $.08	**4** $.16	**5** $.32	**6** $.64	**7** $1.28
8 $2.56	**9** $5.12	**10** $10.24	**11** $20.48	**12** $40.96	**13** $81.92	**14** $163.84
15 $327.68	**16** $655.36	**17** $1,310.72	**18** $2,621.44	**19** $5,242.88	**20** $10,485.76	**21** $20,971.52
22 $41,943.04	**23** $83,886.08	**24** $167,772.16	**25** $335,544.32	**26** $671,088.64	**27** $1,342,177.30	**28** $2,684,354.60

At the end of one month you'll have more than two million dollars! Now that's penny power!

4 YOU 2 Do

Word Play

Add it up! Use the words **savings, spending, deposit,** and **helping** to answer these problems.

CASH + BUYING = _____

CASH + GIVING = _____

CASH + NOT SPENDING = _____

CASH + THE BANK = _____

Making Connections

Beth, Mike, and Rob all had money. But Mike spent *all* his money. He did not save. What could Beth tell Mike about saving?

On Paper

Rob saved for a skate deck. What could you save for? Write a plan that tells how you would save for it. Be sure to tell how you would make money.

Possible answers for Word Play: spending, helping, savings, deposit

Wants and Needs

Fresh

50¢   50¢

Lemonade

Contents

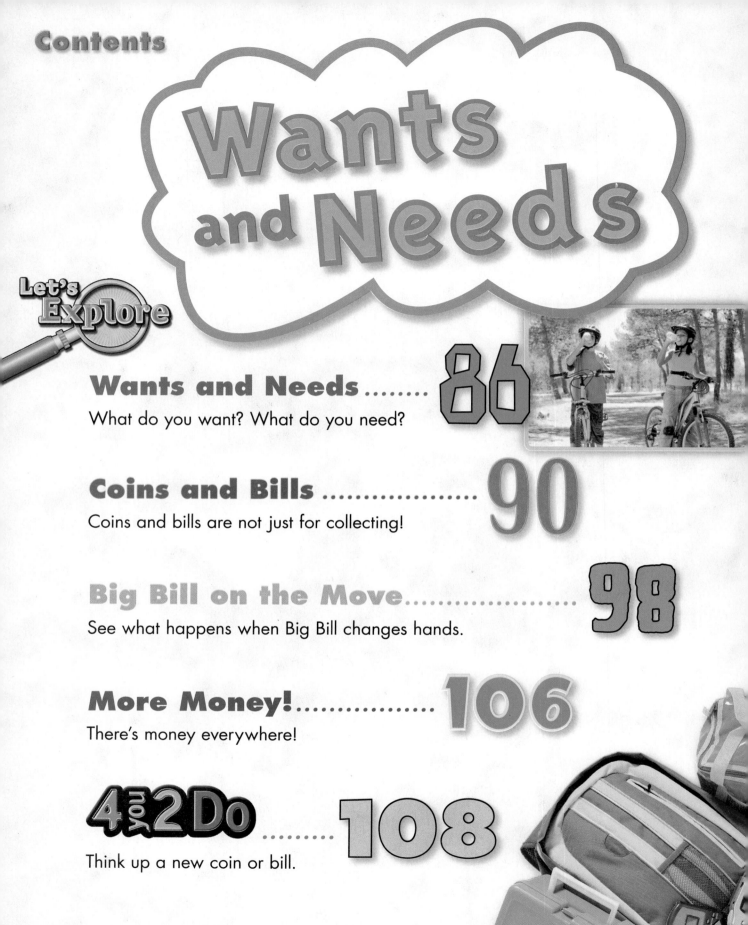

Wants and Needs

Let's Explore

Words 2 the Wise

People need things.
People want things too.
As you read, think about
people's **wants and
needs.**

Let's Explore

Wants

Everyone has wants and needs. Wants are fun things we like to get. Needs are things we must have.

Do you need a kite? Not a bit! Getting a kite is nice, but it is not a need. A kite is a want.

and Needs

Do you need water? You bet! People must drink water. Water is a need. Can a bike be a need? Yes, it can! These kids need bikes to get places when Mom and Dad can not drive them.

How can we get things we want and need? Shopping is one way. But you must have money for shopping. How can you get *that*?

Save this nickel and save that penny. Save those quarters. Save up dollars too. These coins and bills add up to lots of cash!

Are you filling a bank with cash? Have you planned how you will spend it? Will you get things you need or things you want?

Coins and Bills

by Jeff Nakabayashi

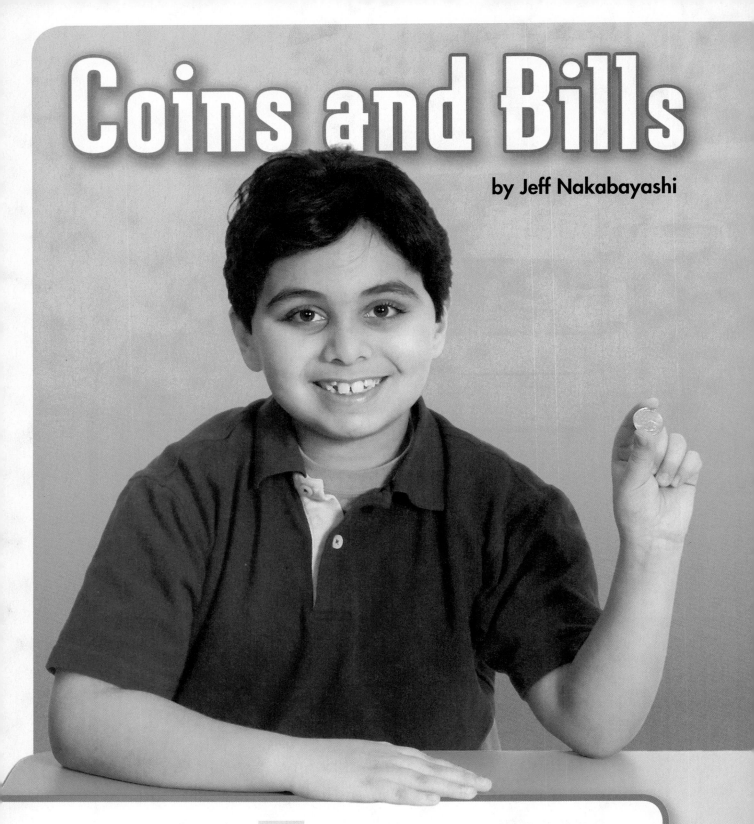

Brad dropped coins in his bank. They landed with a plink, plank, plunk. Brad had saved lots of coins. Brad will use them for shopping.

Which coins did Brad drop in his bank?

Brad dropped in this penny. It is one cent.

Brad dropped in this nickel. A nickel is worth more than a penny. A nickel is five cents.

Brad dropped in this dime. A dime is ten cents. It is worth two nickels.

Brad dropped in this quarter. A quarter is 25 cents. It is worth two dimes and a nickel.

Kate had saved lots of coins too. Like Brad, she will use them for shopping.

Kate and Brad need things for class. Mom will help them get these things. But Kate and Brad want things too. They will use their cash for these things.

Brad and Kate add up their cash. Kate is placing her coins side by side. Brad is piling up his. Did Kate save enough money? Did Brad?

What do Kate and Brad need? What do they want?

Kate needs pens. She must have black pens and red pens for class. Kate would like a cute case for the pens.

Kate *needs* pens. Kate *wants* a cute case for them.

Brad must have black and red pens too. Brad needs a lunch box as well. Brad wants a different backpack and a game.

Brad *needs* pens and a lunch box. He *wants* a backpack and a game.

Needs
black pens
red pens
lunch box
T-shirts
socks
pants

Wants
pen case
backpack
game

Mom is making a list. Mom is writing what Brad and Kate need. Then Mom adds things she thinks the kids need. Next, Mom writes what Brad and Kate want.

Mom, Kate, and Brad will shop for what the kids need first. Then they will shop for what the kids want.

Mom is getting set to shop. She checks her cash. Mom makes sure that she has lots of dollar bills. Mom checks that she has five-dollar bills and ten-dollar bills too.

"Kate and Brad, it is time to go!"

What Do You Think?

Do Brad and Kate have the same wants and needs? How are they the same? How are they different?

BIG BILL on the Move

by Carolina Falls • illustrated by Rémy Simard

"Help! I am stuck!" yelled Big Bill. "Help!"
Big Dollar Bill was in a bit of a fix.* He was flat on his back on the steps of a city bus. He had just been taking a nice ride in a hand. But then the hand dropped him.

*fix difficult situation

"Sir, watch your step!" Bill yelled as a man stepped on him. The man stopped and looked down. Then he grabbed Big Bill and stuffed him in his vest.

"Don't fret.* You will not spend much time here," said a cute little nickel. "Quarter came and left fast."

*fret worry

Just as Nickel spoke, the man stopped in a shop. "That pen is on sale for one dollar," said a woman with a name tag that said Deb.

The man dug in his vest. Out came Big Bill. "So long, Nickel!" Bill yelled.

Bill had fun chatting with other money in the cash box. But then a hand grabbed him.

"Miss, you get a dollar back," said Deb. She handed Bill to a woman with glasses. The woman tossed Bill into an expensive hand bag.

That bag was filled with stuff. Bill felt a bit cramped. But then a hand grabbed him and dropped him in a big pot.

Thump! A penny bopped Bill on the head. Clunk! A quarter nicked* his nose. Coins fell on him like rain.

*nicked made a small cut

Then Bill felt the pot tipping. He was sliding into a sack! A man took the sack to a bank.

The man smiled and said, "I wish to deposit this money." He handed over the sack.

Soon Big Bill was flat on his back in the bank safe.

That safe was not such a bad place. But Bill hoped to get out.

Then Bill got his wish. A woman came and picked him up. Just as she was getting into a city cab, the wind rose. Then zip! Bill went spinning away.

"Help! I am stuck!" yelled Big Bill. "Help!"

A smiling boy raced to grab Big Bill. "A dollar!" he yelled. "What luck! I found a dollar!"

That was just fine with Big Bill. He was set for another trip.

WHAT DO YOU THINK?

How is the beginning of this story like the end of this story? How is it different?

More Money!

Read Together

People all over the world use money. Find out about the money that people in these places use.

Brazil • Real (ray-AHL)
Brazil has more than one hundred kinds of hummingbirds. One of them is shown on this bill.

Egypt • Pound
This bill does not really weigh a pound or even ten! Writing on this money is in Arabic on one side and English on the other.

China • Yuan (YOO-ahn)

On this bill the moon is shining on a lake in China.

Australia • Half Dollar

This half dollar shows that coins don't have to be round!

Europe • Euro (YOO-roh)

Some countries in Europe use the same money. The fronts of their coins look the same, but each country changes the back, like these.

Ireland

France

4 YOU 2 DO

Word Play

These words have more than one meaning. Can you figure out which words answer each riddle?

bill   quarter   bank

What is a container for saving money on the shore of a river?

a _____ on a _____

How much does ¼ of a pizza cost?

a _____ for a _____

What is a dollar with a bird's beak on it?

a _____ with a _____

Making Connections

Think of a coin you have. Tell a story about it. Where has it been? Where might it go next?

On Paper

Draw a new coin or a new bill. Write about the picture you drew.

Answers for Word Play: a bank on a bank; a quarter for a quarter; a bill with a bill

KID

Business

Contents

KID Business

Let's Explore

Words 2 the Wise

Kid business can be fun business. How can a kid have a business? You will find out all about it as you read.

Earning Money

Look at the flakes. Eric lifts and tosses them. He likes to make big white piles. He earns cash. This is his business. What a great idea!

What jobs do his pals like to do?

Emma and Jane like to sell things. It is a hot summer day. They set up a stand.

Emma fills glasses with ice. Then Jane fills the glasses with cold drinks. One glass is 25 cents. Their customers give them money. This is their business.

Shannon likes baking. She bakes many little cakes. Then she puts colored dots on top. Shannon sells the cakes for 75 cents.

Dennis is having a picnic. Shannon fills his basket with ten cakes. Dennis likes this product a lot!

Sam likes riding. He has a business on his bike. He fills his bag. Then Sam rides to homes and hands the news to his customers. This is how he earns cash.

It is fun to earn cash. What job can you do?

Biz Kids

by Amie Jane Leavitt

This is Elise. Elise is a kid with a business. That makes her a Biz Kid. At age three, Elise learned to make fun things to eat. At age ten, she got to sell them. She did this with the help of her big brother.

Elise and her brother Evan

Chocolate Corn Patch

Chocolate Cows

Chocolate Vegetable Garden

Elise made the product. Her brother ran the Web site. Look at the pictures. Yum. These things tasted good. Customers just ate them up!

This business got big fast. So Elise and her brother got pals and workers to help them.

How did Elise and her brother make it happen? They had a plan. If you have an idea for a business, then here is some advice. Like Elise, you must have a plan. Just follow these five steps to make your business a success.

THINK
CHAT
WRITE
MAKE
SELL

Biz Kids must put their thinking caps on! Your business can be fun and a success. But you must find what you are good at first.

Think about things you like. Can you earn money by selling those things? Pick one that will become your product.

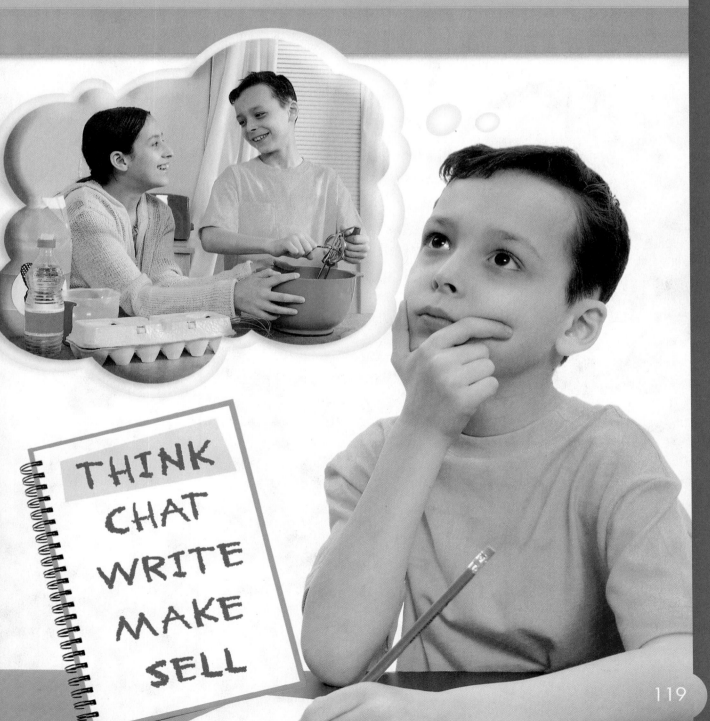

THINK
CHAT
WRITE
MAKE
SELL

You have an idea. Can you just sell? Not yet! It is time to chat!

Chat with people who have businesses you admire. Ask them for hints and learn from their mistakes. Take notes! How can you use what you learned?

The next step in the plan is to write. Biz Kids write lots of notes. What do they write? Biz Kids can write questions that help them plan. They can use an idea web like the one on this page. Biz Kids think about answers and write them down.

How will we make our product?

Who will our customers be?

Our Business

How much will we sell our product for?

What will we name our business?

THINK
CHAT
WRITE
MAKE
SELL

It is time to make your product. Get what you will use. Then get pals to help.

Make it special. Make it stand out. Will it excite people? Can you make your product different from what customers can get in a shop?

THINK
CHAT
WRITE
MAKE
SELL

At last! You have your product! It is time to pack it and sell it. Add the name of your business. Put price tags on the boxes or bags.

You did it! You made a product. You will get customers. You are a Biz Kid!

THINK
CHAT
WRITE
MAKE
SELL

What Do You Think?

Do you have what it takes to be a Biz Kid? How will you do it?

THE DOG WASH

by Sophie Caribacas • illustrated by Suzanne Beaky

Miss Hindale was planning a class trip. "Who would like to go to the Reptile House?" she asked. Every hand in the class shot up.

"Good," said Miss Hindale. "But tickets are expensive. We must earn money for this trip."

Anton waved his hand. "I have an idea for a business," he said. "We can have a dog wash!"

The other kids nodded and smiled. They liked this idea. Miss Hindale did too. She helped the class make a list of things to get.

The class collected five tubs, six brushes, and one hose. They filled a plastic bucket with rags. Chad and Sam made a big sign to stick on the grass. Brendan and Kim handed out notes to people with dogs. Then it was time for a dog wash!

Some kids washed dogs. Miss Hindale hosed the dogs off. Then other kids patted and brushed the dogs. Suds filled the tubs and spilled over the sides. A blanket of suds hid dog noses and legs.

Doctor Candise happened to be driving by
the dog wash. He had his pig Primrose with him.
Primrose was covered in mud. Those suds would
help get rid of that mud. Yes, Doctor Candise was in
luck. These kids were having a hog wash!

Kids rubbed. Dogs yipped and yapped. But an odd grunting came from one tub.

Anna grabbed a wet nose and gave it a rub. "This is not a dog nose!" she said. Then she grabbed a wet leg. "This is not a dog leg!"

Primrose splashed. Dogs ran this way and that. Kids and customers chased them. What a mess!

"Doctor Candise, grab your pig!" yelled Miss Hindale. "You have made a mistake! This is *not* a hog wash!"

Then Anton spoke. "I have an idea," he said. "Will you help, Doctor Candise?"

Soon customers made two lines. In one, people gave dollars for a dog wash. In the other, kids gave quarters to pet a nice fresh pig!

DOG WASH

PET A HOG 25¢

DOG WASH $1

WHAT DO YOU THINK?

Why does Doctor Candise mistake the dog wash for a hog wash?

What can you do with old stuff that you don't want anymore? You can have a yard sale. Customers will come from all over. That's because it costs less to buy something at a yard sale than at a store. How do you do it? Read on.

Steps for Having a Yard Sale

- ☑ Ask if you can have a yard sale. Get other family members to help.

- ☑ Find things you don't use anymore. Ask if you can sell them.

- ☑ Pick a day for your sale. Make posters that tell the time and place.

- ☑ Put a price tag on each item.

- ☑ Get a special box to hold the money.

- ☑ Set up tables and put out the items.

- ☑ Make sure an adult is there!

Have a great yard sale!

4 YOU 2 DO

Word Play

Unscramble the underlined words to read a secret message.

| earn business customer product idea expensive |

Here is a <u>subsines</u> tip. Do you have a great <u>aide</u> for a new <u>dropcut</u>? What is it? If it is not too <u>vixespene</u>, you can <u>rane</u> lots of money. Make a plan and stick to it. Before you know it, you will have your first <u>trocesum</u>.

Making Connections

Think about the kids you read about. What parts of having a business are hard? What parts are fun?

On Paper

Work with a partner. Write a list of ideas for products. Then write who the customers will be. Decide which idea will be the best business.

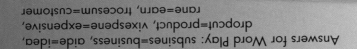

Answers for Word Play: subsines=business, aide=idea, dropcut=product, vixespene=expensive, rane=earn, trocesum=customer

Glossary

al·low·ance (ə lou′ əns), *NOUN.* a sum of money given or set aside for expenses: *My weekly allowance is $5.*

a·mount (ə mount′), *NOUN.* the total sum: *What is the amount of the bill for the groceries?*

at·tend (ə tend′), *VERB.* to be present at: *I will attend my cousin's wedding.* **at·tends, at·tend·ed, at·tend·ing.**

build (bild), *VERB.* to make by putting together materials: *Carpenters build houses.* **built, build·ing.**

busi·ness (biz′ nis), *NOUN.*

1 work done to earn a living; job: *A chef's business is cooking food.*

2 a store, factory, or other place that makes or sells goods and services: *They started a pet-sitting business.* *PL.* **busi·ness·es.**

cen·ter (sen′ tər), *NOUN.* a place where people go for a certain purpose: *We went ice-skating at the recreation center.*

a in hat	ō in open	sh in she
ā in age	o̊ in all	th in thin
â in care	ô in order	ŦH in then
ä in far	oi in oil	zh in measure
e in let	ou in out	ə = { a in about
ē in equal	u in cup	e in taken
ėr in term	u̇ in put	i in pencil
i in it	ü in rule	o in lemon
ī in ice	ch in child	u in circus
o in hot	ng in long	

coin (koin), *NOUN.* a piece of metal used as money: *Pennies, nickels, dimes, and quarters are coins.*

com • mu • ni • ty (kə myü′ nə tē), *NOUN.* a place where people live, work, and play: *Stores, houses, and libraries are all part of a community. PL.* **com•mu•ni•ties.**

cus • tom • er (kus′ tə mər), *NOUN.* a person who buys things in a store: *She gave the customer change.*

de • pos • it (di poz′ it),

    1 *NOUN.* something put in a certain place to be kept safe: *When you put money in the bank, you make a deposit.*

    2 *VERB.* to put in a place to be kept safe: *Deposit your money in the bank.* **de • pos • it • ed, de • pos • it • ing.**

dol • lar (dol′ ər), *NOUN.* an amount of money in the United States and Canada equal to 100 cents: *One dollar is the same as $1.00.*

earn (ėrn), *VERB.* to get money in return for work or service; to be paid: *She will earn $175 a week in her part-time job.* **earned, earn • ing.**

a in hat	ō in open	sh in she
ā in age	ȯ in all	th in thin
â in care	ô in order	ŦH in then
ä in far	oi in oil	zh in measure
e in let	ou in out	⎧ a in about
ē in equal	u in cup	⎪ e in taken
ėr in term	u̇ in put	ə = ⎨ i in pencil
i in it	ü in rule	⎪ o in lemon
ī in ice	ch in child	⎩ u in circus
o in hot	ng in long	

ef•fort (ef′ ərt), NOUN.

    1 the use of concentration and energy to do something; trying hard: *Climbing a steep hill takes effort.*

    2 an attempt to do something: *She did not win the race, but she made an effort.*

ex•pen•sive (ek spen′ siv), ADJECTIVE. costing a lot of money; having a high price: *My uncle has an expensive car.*

goods (gûds), NOUN. personal property; belongings: *The tribes traded goods to get what they needed.*

i•de•a (ī dē′ ə), NOUN. a thought or plan: *It was my idea to go to the zoo.* PL. **i•de•as.**

mon • ey (mun′ ē), *NOUN.* coins and paper used for buying and selling things: *People who work at jobs are paid money.*

nick • el (nik′ əl), *NOUN.* a coin of the United States and Canada worth five cents: *I can buy five one-cent stamps with a nickel.*

pen • ny (pen′ ē), *NOUN.* a coin of the United States and Canada worth one cent: *A nickel and a penny add up to six cents.* *PL.* **pen • nies.**

a in hat	ō in open	sh in she
ā in age	ȯ in all	th in thin
â in care	ô in order	ŦH in then
ä in far	oi in oil	zh in measure
e in let	ou in out	
ē in equal	u in cup	a in about
ėr in term	u̇ in put	e in taken
i in it	ü in rule	ə = i in pencil
ī in ice	ch in child	o in lemon
o in hot	ng in long	u in circus

prod • uct (prod′ əkt), *NOUN.* something that someone makes or grows: *Lemonade is a product that some kids sell during the summer.*

quar • ter (kwôr′ tər), *NOUN.* a coin of the United States and Canada worth twenty-five cents: *One quarter is the same as 25¢ or $.25.*

sav • ings (sā′ vingz), *NOUN PLURAL.* all the money you have saved: *I put my savings in a bank downtown.*

swap (swäp),

    1 *NOUN.* an exchange or trade: *Do you think a marble for a card is a fair swap?*

    2 *VERB.* to trade: *Will you swap books with me?* **swapped, swap·ping.**

trade (trād),

    1 *NOUN.* an exchange: *They made an even trade of baseball cards.*

    2 *VERB.* to give one thing to get another: *Joe asked Bill to trade prizes with him.* **trad·ed, trad·ing.**

worth (wėrth), *ADJECTIVE.* equal in value to: *This book is worth fifteen dollars.*

a in hat	ō in open	sh in she
ā in age	ȯ in all	th in thin
â in care	ô in order	ŦH in then
ä in far	oi in oil	zh in measure
e in let	ou in out	a in about
ē in equal	u in cup	e in taken
ėr in term	u̇ in put	ə = i in pencil
i in it	ü in rule	o in lemon
ī in ice	ch in child	u in circus
o in hot	ng in long	

Acknowledgments

Text

Every effort has been made to locate the copyright owner of material reproduced in this component. Omissions brought to our attention will be corrected in subsequent editions. Grateful acknowledgment is made to the following for copyrighted material.

28 Scott Treimel New York "Lewis Has a Trumpet" by Karla Kuskin from *In the Middle of the Trees*. Copyright © 1959, renewed 1986 by Karla Kuskin. Used by permission of Scott Treimel NY.

29 Simon & Schuster Books for Young Readers "Crazy Boys" by Beverly McLoughland first appeared in *Hand in Hand: An American History Through Poetry*. Edited by Lee Bennett Hopkins, Simon & Schuster, 1994. Used by permission of the author.

Illustrations

2, 12 Margeaux Lucas; **2, 54** Steven Mach; **3, 72–79** Melanie Siegel; **20–27** Maurie Manning; **28, 29** Judith Du Four Love; **34–37** Holli Conger; **38–45, 140** Albert Lorenz; **46–53** Lindy Burnett; **58–63, 80, 81, 136** Jim Steck; **64–71, 139** Ronnie Rooney; **84–97** Chris Lensch; **98–105** Rémy Simard; **124–131** Suzanne Beaky.

Photographs

Every effort has been made to secure permission and provide appropriate credit for photographic material. The publisher deeply regrets any omission and pledges to correct errors called to its attention in subsequent editions. Unless otherwise acknowledged, all photographs are the property of Pearson Education, Inc. Photo locators denoted as follows: Top (T), Center (C), Bottom (B), Left (L), Right (R), Background (Bkgd)

Cover: (CL) ©Bruce Laurence/Getty Images, (CR) ©Image Source/Getty Images, (BR) ©Steffan Hill/Alamy; **1** (CL) ©Charles C. Place/Getty Images; **3** (BR) Thomas Ropke/ Corbis; **5** (C) Terry Vine/Getty Images; **6** (BR) ©Bruce Laurence/Getty Images; **8** (C) ©Steffan Hill/Alamy; **10** (C) ©Blend Images/Alamy; **11** (T) ©Charles C. Place/Getty Images; **30** (BR) ©Bruce Laurence/Getty Images; **31** (CC) ©Stockbyte; **57** (C) Randy Faris/Corbis; **59** (C) Michael A. Keller/Corbis; **82** (BR) Michael A. Keller/Corbis; **83** (C) Getty Images; **84** (CR) ©Image Source/Getty Images; **86** (C) ©Holdman Willie/PhotoLibrary Group, Inc.; **87** (BC) ©Image Source/Getty Images; **88–89** Losevsky Pavel/ Alamy; **89** (BC) ©Dave & Les Jacobs/Getty Images; **108** (BR, BL) S.T. Yiap/Alamy Images; **109** (C) Getty Images; **110** (TR) Jason McConathey/©The Chocolate Farm, Denver, CO, (BR) Jupiter Images; **111** (CL) ©RubberBall/ SuperStock; **112** (CL) Dennis MacDonald/PhotoEdit; **113** (TR) Getty Images; **114** (CL) Lisa Pines/Getty Images; **115** (TR) Yellow dog productions/Getty Images; **116** (T) Jason McConathey/©The Chocolate Farm, Denver, CO; **117** (BR, BL, BC) Jason McConathey/©The Chocolate Farm, Denver, CO, (T) T.S.Webster/©The Chocolate Farm, Denver, CO; **118** (CL) Thomas Ropke/Corbis; **120** (T) Dex Images/Corbis; **121** (C) BananaStock; **122** (T) Getty Images; **123** (T) ©Royalty-Free/Corbis, (T) Tom Stewart/Corbis; **132** (T, BC) Jupiter Images, (T) Thinkstock, (C) TongRo Image Stock; **133** (TR) ©David Sacks/Lifesize/ Thinkstock, (B) ©Ariel Skelley/Blend Images/Getty Images; **134** (BR) ©RubberBall/SuperStock; **137** (T) jupiter/Jupiter Images; **138** (B) ©David Sacks/ Lifesize/ Thinkstock; **142** (C) Getty Images.